This Is What Bodies Do

poems by

Lauren Villa

Finishing Line Press
Georgetown, Kentucky

This Is What Bodies Do

Publisher: Leah Huete de Maines
Editor: Christen Kincaid
Cover Art: Lauren Villa
Author Photo: Alexis Gautier
Cover Design: Elizabeth Maines McCleavy

Order online: www.finishinglinepress.com
also available on amazon.com

Author inquiries and mail orders:
Finishing Line Press
PO Box 1626
Georgetown, Kentucky 40324
USA

Table of Contents

Tiger Fish

It's been 6 hours since I left
I'm alone for the first time in 20 days
I want to ask you questions
Stupid, ordinary questions
I want to annoy you
> *Could you ask her for more*
> *wine the next time she comes down the aisle?*

I want to whisper
> *You were right*
> *I totally should have upgraded*
> *$35 was worth the extra comfort*

You'd say, I told you so
To be honest, I'd give anything
To hear you say that right now
And bite my cheek
I want to complain
About my back and how small these seats are
> *Doesn't this plane feel like it's from the 90s?*
> *Did you hear about the flight where the window ripped off?*

I want to turn and read you a page from my book
> *Tiger fish! Did you know they can bite through regular fishing lines?*

I feel your ghost in these moments
It's still fresh enough
Like I can taste the outline of you
On the empty seat next to me
Pressing itself into the headrest
The fragrance, the feel of you on my clothes

Family members. They're everywhere. In front of me. Behind me. A
husband and wife. A son. A father.
A baby. A grandma.

Their conversations feel like attacks
Do you think they're wondering why we're not here together?
> Wondering why I'm alone, on a plane from the 90s, worrying
> about whether the door will rip off,

Needing the stewardess to pour me more wine and truly
wondering how much you know about
tiger fish.

Everything Soft
After Frank O'Hara

I love you more than anything in the world. I love you for your knowledge of batteries. Gallium nitrate chargers. The way being sick with you is even more fun than going to an elephant orphanage, Mauritius, Portugal, Thailand, or eating seaside in Morocco. It's mostly because of the way you wear shorts that are shorter than short. How you open the car door. How you look happiest when the buttons on your most colorful shirt are down like you're going to a disco at any moment. Mostly because you spritz the end of that bottle you know is my favorite scent. How you knock on the door, say the magic password, still taste like the perfume of hibiscus and bougainvillea from outside. Because you stick the incense into an orange at the house by the river. Some men give roses, but you grill meat and hand me a hot drumstick. I love you because you bounce to the sound of rain and remind the bartender that I wanted pink tonic with my gin, not the regular kind. Mostly though, because of your big brown eyes and the sorcery of waking up next to you. How you pluck the frangipanis off the ground, dust the dirt off of them, take a look, and tuck them behind my ear before we head off to the restaurant. How you refuse to hug me harder because you want everything you do to my body to be soft. I wish I had the gift of time travel. It's hard to believe we live on this twirling, swirling planet going about 1,000 miles an hour when you have the power to stop time and fill my cells with more delight in the span of a few days than anyone could within 1,000 years. Partly because you continue to love me like this despite my outbursts. I look at pictures of you and it makes me mad for a moment. That you are you and that God created such a fine piece of art, that I have spent so much time with people that I didn't love.

The Art of Travel

I had no idea that losing my passport, delaying the trip,
would be the weird, swirly staircase leading to you

I have legs without knees, knees without cartilage
but still climbed the steps, finally entered this world

the space in time where I find you is the shape of a palm tree.
       The shape of a hotel: at night. Tropical.

But by then,
I was wearing a black dress, patent heels, even though I couldn't
stand

pearls— balancing up a gin, tonic, a sausage roll.
I whispered, *What was that?* Pointing,

so you'd come closer and talk to me.

Crocodiles

You're wedged
into every part
of my California.
Even the new
leather couch.

How Did You Meet?

What would he do if he was here now?
> *He'd hold up an avocado and say "it's perfect, like
> an avocado emoji. Even this," and twist the seed, rotate
> it in its green pocket. He'd look back and say, "You
> never get that."*

What's his hair like?
> *A mass of stars.*

How do you deal with the distance?
> *I split my brain in two.*

Why's that?
> *One to daydream about our future, the other to
> function with the reality that time is slipping through
> my fingers like beach sand.*

So what are you guys going to do?
> *Become hummingbirds. Like Animorphs.*

What do you mean?
> *Hummingbirds can fly forwards and backwards. They
> can hover! They can even fly upside-down.*

I don't get it.
> *I don't blame you.*

Ruth

Today I had to buy things that I love,
I had to leave my house, to wander
through the little stores, the ones
curated, perfect. Where the floors
are swept and women named Ruth
man the counter. I had to get a small
something wrapped in tissue
paper, Ruth had to ask if I want
a punch card and where I was from.

One Boy

Sleeping together in this bed
Finding skin to burrow into
Like we're one boy

Glow Gold

It almost makes me mad
how hot I find you, almost
gets me in trouble when
I think about what's happening
between us, almost makes me
glow gold, I try to forget how
you killed the spider crawling
above my head, sleeping
in that house filled with bugs,
all kinds, bug hotel, huge white
moths, tiny ants, beetles with horns.
Bugs like the light, so we switch
everything off, when I have to go
to the bathroom, I run on tip toe over
their tiny exoskeletons, praying I don't
step on them, crunch, then back into
bed, as fast as I can, a woman
half-eaten, you pick up the remote
to turn the AC down as low as it will
go, 17 degrees celsius, but all night
the one and the seven glow, while
the bugs nibble away.

Red-Winged Starling

The bush is like Arizona, kind of. It's kind
of like the desert, kind of like a border town,
wild with bones, skulls laying around there too,
the sun melts and there are dogs, wild dogs
wearing turquoise earrings, and if you spend enough
time there, enough time in the bush, or the desert,
one day you'll find yourself saying things like,
is that a red-winged starling? Watch out. Rattlesnake.

Mustard Seed

I never quite understood what
a mustard seed was supposed to be.
What I was supposed to do when
they talked about it in church, have faith
of a mustard seed, they said, but how
can something so tiny symbolize faith?
To be honest, I don't even know what
a mustard seed looks like, to this day I
haven't Googled mustard-seed-size,
or read the story, is it in the Bible?
I could look it up, but it's interesting
not to know something that everyone
else seems to know. However, I *would*
like to know if I have faith
of a mustard seed, if that's what this is.

Pocket Guide Birds of Zambia

First, you need to know where you are
The season you're in

You need to know what they sound like, the color of their feathers,
        the shape of their bill, beak, how they fly when they fly

There's a way to read the handbook, a whole art to identifying their
calls, male or female,
        breeding, non breeding

It's only then, when you hold out the tiny pictures, diagram of a
wingspan, that you yell out from
        the porch, baby, it's a Hornbill Trumpeter!

Shhhh, be quiet, I don't want it to fly away, look that's what was sitting
there all along, red-eyed, crying
        like a cat, crying like a baby all night long, going "waah,
        waah, waah."

When I Was 10 Years Old I Made a Replica of a Solar System

Bought a packet of acrylic multicolored pom-poms
superglued them to styrofoam balls
hung them with invisible fishing wire
painted the back of a shoebox black
poured handfuls of glitter onto globs of Elmer's
to make stars, galaxies, milky ways
using decorative scissors to cut the labels for each planet
proudly placing the shoebox at the front of the class
so everyone could take a look

Falling in love with you was like that

When everyone sees what we created
they come out of their houses
out of apartments, coffee shops, leaving their laptops open
they come out of galleries and bus stops to go AWWWWWWWW
when you witness someone falling in love you have to stop and take a
look

Since You Asked

I think everything comes in season. When it's ready. Like fruit or vegetables or wheat. Like how he parked in a handicap spot when he picked me up from the airport, sprinkled rose petals over the bed, the truth is, it's so much easier to see now that the best part was our evening walk, making a vase out of a hotel ice bucket, popping holes in the triangular milk cartons and spilling the milk onto a plate for the kittens in the garden to lap up, it was even better than your "welcome back to Lusaka rain," better than the earth spilling out, morning meditations, hands on the green trunk of the tree, covered in moss, blindfolded for a minute as I pulled the shirt up over my head, better than the ambassador running over the champagne bottle, popping tires, jumping into pools, better than watching the guinea fowl lay one egg a day. Since you asked, yes. It was better than I expected. Should I keep going?

Chickens

Through the markets, on the side of the road,
        five chickens sunbathing—white feathers

pyramids of cabbage
the same fabric for holding babies
as for skirts, pillowcases,

it's like a painting:

at this time of year
the whole country turns emerald

it's all green, really
so in any direction, there's a present

waiting, another place where you can cross

the street, let your hair down to dry on your shoulders
you can't get over the amount of green
or the way the sun looks when it hits

this point in the sky and, still,
night ahead—purple, jasmine, flowers—

you drink it all.
In San Diego, the sides
of the highway are covered in green too—it just rained, flooded parts of
the city

        you have to remind yourself it's just as glittering here too, that
        there are still chickens sunbathing, somewhere.

Looks More Like Stir Fry Than Pad Thai

Making pad thai
in my apartment is cold
it's lonely, I don't think
the insulation works
this is date night or date breakfast
my recipe isn't working out
I think I soaked the rice noodles too long
the ones I bought late night
drove to 99 Ranch Market because
the lady at Trader Joes said
sorry, we don't carry oyster sauce
this is what long distance feels like
me in a beanie and crocs standing
in front of my stove waiting for chicken to brown
cutting up chives, whisking brown sugar
soy sauce, oyster sauce, fish sauce
taking selfies
   I wish you were here
   I love you
waiting for the noodles to cool so I can throw
them in with the rest of the ingredients
to be honest, it doesn't look good
it comes out looking like big mush
but I eat it for breakfast anyway

Wires

What will I have for breakfast? Honestly,
I'd like your lips, right now I want them
soft to mine, galvanized, oxidized, copper
like copper mines, mining for millions, millions
of pounds of precious, precious metals. Your lips
they're hammering out a sentence now, over the phone,
hot, sparking, easily conducting millions of miles away,
your lips are hammering out a sentence that flows in, then
out of me, through me, hot current, jumps out of the phone
wraps around my neck, golden, like wire, romantic as a movie,
romantic as True Romance, the sentence, the line, it's about where
we go from here, and I ground into it, softly from your lips to mine.

Playing Battleship in Swimsuits

You're with your friends eating KFC
celebrating birthdays
but do you remember when
we watched the hippos all morning
their heads popped up
two of them
we didn't know they were there
unlike the birds and the monkeys
the hippos slide up and down the Zambezi
one of them comes up from the water
slow as well, a hippo
we watch until the sun sets
play battleship in our swimsuits
listening to the
grunts, roars, honks, and wheezes
the muuaaaaarrrhhhh
I wish I could hear it now
the backdrop of defending what's yours
the open mouth of swallowing everything beautiful

Patrick Bentley

I'm going to pull out the photographer's book
that's sitting on the shelf.

A black and white image
of a lioness waiting for something to happen.

Her eyes say, "I've been following you."
After I have experienced the bush

to the fullest, to the very core of my being,
I will flip through these photographs,

wrap my head in morning mist
like the day I saw her, behind a tree,
her huge mysteriousness, skin cracked
with laugh lines, she's watching, and still now

that elephant shakes my entire living room
with each heavy step, reminding me of what I love.

It's True What They Say

Things can change in a day. One day you're renovating a house in North Carolina and the next you're curled under a kiss that billows like a sail-ship dream over your lips. Let it. You melt inside the oven of his mouth, feeling the current of magic enter you like a big, blue genie, like rubbing a magic lamp, like you immediately need to feel your waist wrapped by his hands, like he's hugging the trunk of a tree and you're hollow, what's up is down, something is coming unhinged, the sudden rhinoceros of his nose into your neck and the looping and swooping and dipping and soaring of your heart inside of a hollow body. You swell with gallons of blood pumping until it finally falls like a fat, ripe lime off the tree. Unhinged from the branch. And what tumbles towards your feet is green. It's life and hope and you open up like something that was covered by moss, hidden by ferns. Just like that castle (well it's not really a castle it's a mansion which is a modern day castle right?) that you pass on your morning walks by the ocean, the one with the tall iron gates and the courtyard no one ever uses where the windows are sealed shut with a metal padlock, where rain thuds against the brass-studded windows, green climbing ivy and bursts of wisteria, so that strangers, you know drifters from the street don't come inside. Instead of hurrying and scurrying away, you cut away the ivy, open the windows, let the morning sun in, let him in, put on your hat, hop in a boat and cross the river, to find what's on the other side. Beside the boat there's fish bigger than you've ever imagined. Its rainbow scales are like the ones in your favorite children's book. Your heart pounds the entire boat ride, until you reach the other side, where to your surprise, he's still there, but now there's also moon, driftwood, jasmine, and purple earthworms wrapping themselves around your trunk.

So Much Left To Do

The shadows have come back, casting onto the kitchen
   cabinets, underneath the espresso maker, where black grounds
   run away from me. But as much as I try to clean, things can't find
   their place. The dishwasher fills with liquid, the soap pod

   refuses to fly out of it's trap door, in a week I'll finally figure it out:
   The setting was on Rinse Only. Time passes. I buy paint, but the
color
   is too dark. It chalks the wall, turning my house into a cave. My
mailbox
   #21 of 65 in the complex, is jammed, so I have no choice but to
leave the key

   hanging. I call Dupe-A-Key. It's cold, but I open the windows,
sleep with the
   air purifier running. The painters come on Monday, Tuesday,
Wednesday
   to fix the mess I made, straighten out the edges, redo the crown
   molding. Patch the holes. They leave nails I hammered for
pictures

   even though I ask them to remove them. Under the covers, I call
you,
   you're getting ready for work, your dog is in the background:
   her little face resting in the place where you were sleeping,
probably
   because it smells like you, probably because it's still warm.

   There's no way I can get to you fast enough. No way. Your bed
would
   be cold. It would be a different day entirely. It takes at least 40
hours
   to fly across the world. Besides, I still need to organize everything
   under the sink. Fix the shower head. Hang curtains. So much left
to do.

Love In The Time of Trash Day

All the beautiful poems about traveling the world,
living a big, fat, creative life. All the poems about
marriage, babies, crying on your closet floor. All
the books about breaking through, Oprah interviews,
all the podcasts turned to 1.5x speed telling you to
follow your heart! Sell your stuff! Jump off the cliff!
All the Audible book titles like UNTAMED, WE CAN DO HARD
THINGS, BIG MAGIC, YOU ARE A BADASS, SPIRITUAL BABIES,

and not one of them mentions
the reality that I keep
missing trash day,
I keep missing your call.
A perfect wall
of flattened cardboard
sits by my front door.

The padlock is on the dumpster so I wait until someone else unlocks
it. I can't be bothered on a Saturday morning and I hate the clanking
of the lock against the metal can. Especially when the weather is this
nice and the sun is finally out.

None of those poems or books or podcasts talk about how your
neighbor yells at you for putting the cardboard in the wrong
dumpster, how you pull out the soggy stuff and throw it into the
dumpster on the left, labeled recycling. You're doing your part.
Maybe this is your big magic.

But no. None of those poems or books or podcasts talk about
the stuff oozing on your hands, the trash juice, the loud sound of
the dumpster shutting, about standing in the middle of the alley,
surrounded by palm trees and flooded driveways, dogs stopping to
drop fresh poop on grass.

They don't talk about your phone buzzing in your pocket, wiping
your hand on the side of your yoga pants to answer as quickly as you
can.

This is What Long Distance Feels Like

When you realize you're not special, that this isn't necessarily about you, that it's more about physics,

> you'll know that's when it started. It doesn't have any solutions or timelines to give you. It has something to show you, so it will leave you standing in the middle of the beach, wondering how you ever felt good. You'll want to bury your face in its fragrance, but there won't be a smell there. You'll fall asleep, thinking you see brown eyes, but there aren't any eyes there. It doesn't have eyes. You want to wrap yourself around it, but you slip off, like the side of a wet rock, you hit the sand hard as a belt. It whips its head through the air. Nothing will ever feel this hard. With nothing to press against, you hold the phone tighter. Press it into your cheek until it leaves a mark. When the rain stops you realize you're playing against yourself. You're playing against something softer than air.

Hummingbirds

Just sitting here
still

reflecting
on how they fly upright

facing the world
most birds fly flat

that's it, kiss me hard
on the lips, upright

kiss me now
remember all we did,

how we made love
upright, never flat.

Emerald Season

Blooms of jacaranda
spiraling upwards like
painted toenails, like nature hanging
in a hammock, her feet to the sky, draping
her body over the street, holding handfuls of young
blue-green leaves, letting them fall, folding her arms full
of blue bells, her dress lifting with the wind, climbing up the gate,
bougainvillea drawing her eye up the sides of the house until she
exhales all the way to the tree-tops.

Warthogs

We saw them just as the sun began to squeeze itself
over the dark rim of morning. A female warthog
with her piglet, trotting across the sun-roasted sand.
Did you know piglets spend the first weeks of their lives
underground in burrows? When they're old enough they
come to the surface, follow the mother around, sprint
as fast as they can. I watch the piglet, her mother,
feeling as though I could break into sprint, too.

Hand-off

I don't blame you
I really don't
The woman is nursing right before yoga class
Slips her breast back under her sports bra
"This will be the longest hour of my life.
It's the most time I've spent away from him."
She hands off the newborn to her mom
Yes, she's talking about being a baby
Away from her baby
And I sit here, wondering about you

This Is What Bodies Do

We should be arguing over who's turn it is to tie a tiny knot, throw out the diaper by now.

I should be shopping online for things practical in another body: The Softest Rib Nursing Mini Dress, The 24/7 Feeding Jumpsuit —With easy feeding access, front patch pockets.

We dream about that life, but will the dream ever start? It's winter in San Diego: I keep missing the farmer's market, the beaches are flooding, I need to replace my shower head but I'm too scared I'll break something.

For months now, hiking, walking, or driving, passing a mom and her baby, they're sitting at breweries, ordering tacos, making nests out of blankets and nursing pillows.

This is what bodies do. And yesterday, I ran out of sunscreen, I couldn't find my hat, I walked along the bay and then to the ocean, without a layer of goop or shade, so, a trail of freckles cocooned, hatched.

Again I thought it, in the shower, washing off the sun: This is the best thing bodies do. Rinse hair. Wash out the sun and sweat. Birth.

But now it feels so far, and yet, there are times sitting on the leather couch, when, out of the corner of my eye, I see the hummingbird, the one with the coppery sides and the emerald chest
> *gorgeous*, she's still here, with her two white eggs, draping her body over the nest, to cover, to protect, and I am speechless: I've never seen anything that looks so easy.

Raised in Pinetop, Arizona, **Lauren Villa** is a poet and author of the chapbooks *This Is What Bodies Do* and *Close To Something Beautiful*. She is a graduate of the Writing Seminars program at Johns Hopkins University and the Kenyon Writers Workshop in Gambier, Ohio. She is the recipient of the Gates Millennium Scholarship and the creative fellowship from the Gullkistan Center for Creativity in Iceland. Her work has been nominated for a Pushcart Prize. She is a yogi and currently at work on a collection of poetry titled *Pocha* where she writes about her experience growing up as a Mexican-American who doesn't speak Spanish.

www.ingramcontent.com/pod-product-compliance
Lightning Source LLC
Chambersburg PA
CBHW022100080426
42734CB00009B/1435